The Collector

Peter Viney

Garnet
Oracle

Garnet
EDUCATION

Peter Viney – author of this book, and Series Editor of the Garnet Oracle Readers – has over 40 years' experience teaching English and writing ELT materials. He now combines his writing with lecturing and teacher-training commitments internationally. He has authored and co-authored many successful textbook series and developed a wide range of highly popular video courses. Peter has been series editor and author on a number of graded reader series, and has also published with Garnet Education the highly popular *Fast Track to Reading*.

Published by
Garnet Publishing Ltd
8 Southern Court
South Street
Reading RG1 4QS, UK

www.garneteducation.com

Copyright © Garnet Publishing Ltd 2014

ISBN 978 1 90757 531 0

Photocopying and duplication
The resources in the additional resources section may be photocopied for use by the purchasing institution and the students in its classes. They may not be copied for use by staff or students in other institutions. The CDs may not be duplicated under any circumstances.

British Cataloguing-in-Publication Data
A catalogue record for this book is available from the British Library.

Production

Series editor:	Peter Viney
Editorial: ·	Clare Chandler, Lucy Constable
Design and layout:	Mike Hinks
Illustration:	Bob Moulder
Photographs:	iStockphoto, Shutterstock

Every effort has been made to trace copyright holders and we apologize in advance for any unintentional omission. We will be happy to insert the appropriate acknowledgements in any subsequent editions.

Printed and bound in Lebanon by International Press: interpress@int-press.com

1 August 1ˢᵗ

So, this is a supermarket. It's very big. There aren't any supermarkets at home. We don't need them now.

Everything is cheap here. That's because it's all new. Look at this! Kellogg's Corn Flakes, £2.59! I can sell this packet at home for 5,000 units, maybe 6,000. But I don't want this one. It's got a picture from *Star Trek* on it. I'm looking for a Kellogg's Corn Flakes packet, but I need the 500 gram packet with a dinosaur picture on the back. Those packets are from July and August 2014. It's August 1ˢᵗ, 2014 today.

The twenty-first-century film *Dinosaur Days* is in the cinemas this week. It's a new film and the pictures of dinosaurs are on everything. They're on packets of cornflakes and they're in magazines. All these packets here have got the *Star Trek* picture. Maybe I can ask. There's a young woman near the packets of coffee. She's taking more packets of coffee from a box. She's wearing a green coat. She works in this supermarket. I can ask her.

Me	Excuse me, madam.
Woman	Sorry?
Me	Excuse me, madam. I'm looking for the cornflakes.
Woman	They're over there. You're standing next to them.
Me	You don't understand. I don't want those packets. I want a packet with a dinosaur picture. A 500 gram packet.
Woman	Oh! For your children. They all love *Dinosaur Days*.
Me	Yes. That's right. For my children. They love the film.
Woman	We haven't got any. We're going to get some tomorrow. Come back then.
Me	Tomorrow? What time?
Woman	The food arrives at six o'clock or seven o'clock in the morning. We open at eight.
Me	Thank you, madam.
Woman	Are you English?
Me	Er ... no, I'm not ... I'm a ... I'm a visitor. Why?
Woman	You say strange things. 'Madam'. No one says 'madam' in a supermarket.
Me	I'm sorry.
Woman	Don't be sorry. It's nice.

This is terrible. Can I wait for tomorrow? I don't like it here. It's cold and dirty. And my arm is hurting. But I need that packet. I can get 300,000 units for that packet at home. The dinosaur picture on that packet is by Kate Hermann. She's a very famous artist at home. Many people collect food packets with her pictures on them, but they haven't got the dinosaur picture. Everybody wants that picture. Kate Hermann's picture is famous because the colours of the dinosaurs are correct. Dinosaur pictures usually have all the colours wrong. We know that now.

2 What is she doing here?

Woman Clinton! Hi. How are you?

I know her. Tilda Birdsong. What is she doing here? I don't like her. Does she want a cornflakes packet, too?

Me	I'm fine, thanks. How are you, Tilda?
Tilda	You're looking for something, Clinton. What is it this time?
Me	Nothing.
Tilda	You can tell me! We're friends.
Me	Friends? Are we?
Tilda	Well, our jobs are the same. We're collectors. We buy and sell things.
Me	Why are you here?
Tilda	Why not? It's a twenty-first-century shop. It's an interesting place.
Me	But why today? Why on August 1st, 2014?
Tilda	Maybe I'm hungry. Or thirsty.
Me	What do you want?
Tilda	I've got it. It's here.

There's a packet of tea in her hand. What make is it? Ah, yes. Twinings English Breakfast tea. One pound ninety-nine pence. Expensive, yes. It's a beautiful packet. It's black, gold and yellow. Maybe she can get 20,000 units for that packet back at home, but no more than that. Many collectors have got 2014 Twinings tea packets. But why is she here at the same time, on the same day and in the same place? Does she want the same cornflakes packet, too?

Tilda	When are you going home?
Me	I don't know. Tomorrow, I think.
Tilda	You're not going to sleep here? Here in Britain?

Me	Yes. I think so.
Tilda	Have you got all the right vaccinations?

My arm is hurting. Yes, I have all the vaccinations. You need twenty-three vaccinations for twenty-first-century Britain. Twenty-three. That's not too bad. What about the sixteenth century? The time of William Shakespeare? Don't ask me! You don't want to know! Tilda is looking at me.

Tilda	But where are you going to sleep, Clinton?
Me	In a hotel.
Tilda	Have you got one hundred pounds in British money? A room in a hotel is one hundred pounds.

She's laughing. She's laughing at me. Of course we can't get British banknotes. There isn't any old paper money at home. I have three one pound coins. That's all. You pay about 1,000 units for an old one pound coin. That's why we can buy only one or two things in the supermarket.

Me	It's August. I can sleep outside.
Tilda	It's raining, Clinton. Why don't you go home today? You can come back tomorrow.

She knows the answer. Travelling is expensive, and it's always a little dangerous. We can only travel one day in every month. And we always need to travel home between places.

Tilda	You're waiting for something! I know. It's something important. And it's going to be here tomorrow.

I don't want to tell her about the packet and the Kate Hermann picture of the dinosaurs. It's my information. I work for many days to find information like this – the correct time and place for expensive antiques.

Tilda	OK, Clinton. Don't tell me. You can tell me next week.
Me	Next week?
Tilda	Clinton! Next week is the antiques festival! You're going to be there!

Oh, yes. I'm going to be there. And I'm going to have a very special antique with me. An August 2014 Kellogg's Corn Flakes packet with the *Dinosaur Days* picture. I'm going to get 300,000 units! Maybe more. Tilda's going.

Tilda	Well, goodbye. Don't get too cold tonight!

3 I need some money

I walk out of the supermarket. There are hundreds of cars in the car park. A 2014 car is fifty million units at home. But the cars are all too big. You can't take them with you. Some of the cars are very beautiful ... Toyota Yarises, Suzuki Splashes, Ford Kas, Nissan Micras, Renault Clios, Minis. They're the expensive ones, the everyday cars. You can find Rolls-Royces, Mercedes, Ferraris and Porsches at home. People are always careful with old cars like those. But you can't find these everyday cars.

It's raining hard and I haven't got a coat. And I haven't got much money. Only three pounds. And I need that for the cornflakes tomorrow. The rain is cold.

A young man is sitting on the ground outside the supermarket. He's wearing old, dirty jeans and an old T-shirt. There's a hat in front of him and a sign. The sign says, 'No home. Cold, hungry and thirsty. Please help.' A young woman walks past. She stops, and puts a fifty pence coin in the hat. Then an old man puts a few twenty pence coins in the hat. That's the answer!

A woman is walking along the street. I stop her.

Me   Excuse me. I'm hungry and thirsty. And I'm cold. Please help me.

The woman is looking at my clothes. They're very good clothes. I always get good clothes. I'm wearing an expensive grey suit, new black shoes and a clean white shirt. The woman doesn't say anything. She walks away. Then the young man stands up. His jeans are very dirty. He's angry.

Young man   Hey! You! This is my place! I'm here every day. Go away!

Me   I'm sorry. Don't be angry. I need some money, too.

Young man   Go on! Go away!

He's very angry. And he's a big, strong young man, too. What can I do? I go away. I walk between the cars in the car park. An old man is opening his car door.

Me   Excuse me, sir. I need some money.

The old man is afraid. Why?

Me   Could you give me some money, please?
Old man   Don't hurt me!
Me   I don't want to hurt you. I'm only
              asking a question. Could I have some
              money, please?
Old man   Help! Police! Help!

People are looking at me. The man is running away between the cars. He's shouting. Now a police car is stopping outside the supermarket. Two police officers get out, a man and a woman. The man is talking to them. They're all looking at me. I don't want to talk to the police officers. I run fast between the cars. I can run very fast. I run out of the car park and along a road. There are some trees on my left. I go behind a tree and stop. The police car goes past. The police officers are in the front and the man is in the back seat. They're looking out of the windows. They're looking for me.

4 Fast food

Half an hour later. The police car isn't here now. And it isn't raining. It's the afternoon. I'm hungry. Where can I get some food? There's a restaurant near the supermarket. It has big red and yellow signs outside. They say 'Fast Food'. Maybe I can get some food there.

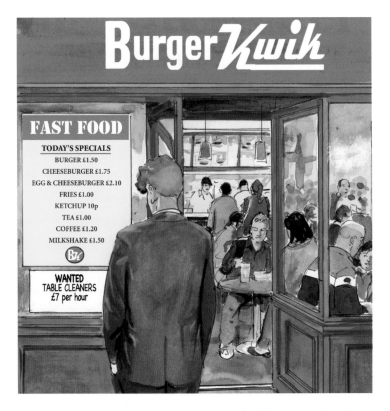

The restaurant is expensive. Well, it's expensive for me. It sells burgers. I need to be careful about twenty-first-century food. Maybe I can't eat burgers. My arm is still hurting from the vaccinations, but the vaccinations don't work for bad food.

Usually you don't eat anything in the twenty-first century. My three one pound coins are in my hand. I need £2.59 for tomorrow so I can get the cornflakes. What can I buy for forty-one pence? The menu is short. Burger, cheeseburger, fries, ketchup, tea, coffee, milkshake. There's nothing for forty-one pence. Well, there's ketchup for ten pence. But I can't eat only ketchup!

There's a small sign in the window.

WANTED TABLE CLEANERS £7 per hour

Seven pounds for one hour! That's fantastic! Maybe I can work for one or two hours. Then I can buy some fries – a lot of fries. Fries and ketchup and a milkshake! And tomorrow I can buy two packets of cornflakes, or maybe three! I walk into the restaurant. There's a young woman near the door. She's wearing a white coat. There's ketchup on the coat and milkshake and tea. There's a sign on her coat, too. It says, 'Linda. Manager'.

Me	Excuse me, madam. Are you Ms Linda Manager?
Linda	Well, my name's Linda, and yes, I'm the manager. Can I help you?
Me	Yes. I want a job. And seven pounds an hour. I can work for two hours or maybe three.
Linda	You? You're not a table cleaner! Not in that suit!

I look down at my suit. Maybe an expensive suit isn't the right thing for 2014.

Me	I can clean tables very well.
Linda	But the job's for a week. Seven pounds an hour. Thirty-five hours a week. That's £245. But we need a table cleaner for a week … not for two or three hours.

A week! In this cold, dirty country! How can they live here?

Linda	But we are busy today ... do you want two hours work?
Me	Oh, yes, please! Very much!
Linda	OK. Come and get a coat.

We go into a small room. There are a lot of white coats. I take my jacket off, and I put it on a seat. I put on a white coat. It isn't very clean. There's ketchup and milkshake and some egg and burger on it.

Linda	You put the dirty things in there and clean the tables. That's all.

The first table is very dirty. There are some dirty paper cups, an old magazine and there's some tea and coffee and sugar and ketchup on the table. There's something under my shoe. It's a fry. A cold French fry. I'm cleaning the table very well.

Linda	What are you doing?
Me	I'm cleaning the table. It's hard work.
Linda	No! Take the dirty things off the table and clean it fast. Like this!
Me	It isn't very clean.
Linda	It's OK!

I put the dirty things in black bags. It's strange. Some of the things are very expensive at home. There are packets and cups with pictures. I put one ketchup packet and some sugar packets in my pocket. White sugar and brown sugar. I work for two hours. Linda isn't happy with me.

Linda	You can go. We aren't very busy now. Here's seven pounds.
Me	The sign says, 'Seven pounds an hour'. I want more money. I want fourteen pounds!
Linda	Seven pounds an hour. That's for a week. Then you pay tax and everything. Seven pounds is all I'm going to pay you. And you can have a burger. Free.

We're in the small room. It's Linda Manager's office. Linda Manager is giving me a blue banknote and a two pound coin. A banknote! I take the dirty white coat off.

Me   Where's my jacket? It isn't on the seat.

Linda   No, it isn't. Anyone can come in here. And it's an expensive jacket. It's behind the door. It's over there.

I go to the door. I take my jacket and put it on. Linda is watching me.

Linda   OK. You can go and get a free burger.

Me   Can I have fries, too?

Linda   All right. Fries, too.

5 Outside

I'm outside under the trees. It's evening. The burger isn't very good, but I'm going to eat it. I hope it's OK. The fries are cold. I don't like them. Twenty-first century food is terrible, and maybe the meat is dangerous for us. But I've got the blue banknote and a two pound coin. I can buy three packets of cornflakes. I'm rich!

~

I can't sleep. It's three o'clock in the morning and I can't sleep. I can hear a dog. It's angry. I'm afraid of dogs. They're dangerous. We don't have dogs at home. Not now. It's cold under the trees. I'm standing up and walking around. I'm very tired. The supermarket opens at eight o'clock. Five more hours!

~

I've got three packets of cornflakes and a black, gold and yellow Twinings English Breakfast tea, because maybe Tilda knows something. And it's only eight-thirty in the morning. I've got two supermarket bags (they're green and red with the 'FoodCo' name), some ketchup, some sugar and some small coins. The bags are free, but they're 6,000 units at home. Now I'm going back to my time machine. In ten minutes I'm going to be back at home in 2561. In 2561 it's always hot, and everything is clean, and there aren't any dogs. In 2561 the food is good, and we don't eat burgers – ergh!

So, where's my time machine? You can't see it. I can't see it, but it's here, in the same place. I leave the time machine only one minute into the future. It's here, near the trees, but it's always one minute in front of us in time. That's why you can't see it. It's waiting for me. I have a small remote control. The control stops the time machine. Then I wait for one minute and the time machine is here. Then I can go home.

Right, take the remote control … but it isn't here! It isn't in my jacket pocket. But why? It isn't in any of my pockets. It's lost! No remote control, no time machine! I'm here, in cold, dirty, dangerous 2014 Britain and I can't leave.

In 2561 my three packets of cornflakes are nearly a million units. Here? They're only breakfast, that's all. Only breakfast, and I haven't got any milk!

Glossary

These extra words are not in the 400 words for Level 1.

antique an old thing that is now very expensive

arm part of the body; your hand is at the end of your arm

artist someone who paints pictures: *Picasso was a famous artist*

banknotes paper money

breakfast the first meal of the day

century 100 years; 1901–2000 is the twentieth century; 2001–2100 is the twenty-first century

coin round metal money

collect get and keep things that you like. People collect antiques, pictures, books, CDs, dolls and many other things

collector a person who collects something: *She is a DVD collector.*

colour red, blue, green, yellow are colours

cornflakes a breakfast food made from pieces of corn. You eat them with milk – Kellogg's Corn Flakes is the most famous make

country Britain, France, USA, Brazil are countries

dangerous something is dangerous if it can hurt you or kill you: *Alligators are very dangerous; That road is dangerous. The cars are going too fast*

festival something that happens on a special day or time every year; there are music festivals (the Glastonbury Festival), film festivals (the Cannes Film Festival); Christmas is a festival on 25th December in Britain

fry, fries potatoes cut in long, thin pieces and cooked in oil

jacket a short coat

magazine a paper, usually in colour. You buy a magazine every week or every month

million 1,000,000

packet a paper box or bag; things in shops are often in packets: *A packet of tea; A packet of cornflakes*

pay when you buy something, you pay the shop with money

pocket jackets and trousers have pockets. You can put money, keys, etc., in a pocket

remote control you have a remote control for TVs or for car doors; it turns a TV on and off or locks and unlocks car doors

same not different; a thing like another thing: *These books are both dark blue. They're the same colour; My sister and I live in the same house*

sign a sign gives you information. The information can be in words, or in pictures: *The road sign says, 'Paris 250 kilometres'; There's a sign on the door, with a picture of a man*

suit jacket and trousers (or skirt) made of the same material in the same colour

supermarket a large shop which sells food (and other things like books, cards and items for houses)

tax money you pay every year to your country: *I get £500 a week. I pay 25% tax to my country;* also money you pay when you buy things: *The tax in shops here is 20%*

terrible very bad

time machine something that can move you in time, from the past to the future or from the future to the past. Time machines are only in books or films

travel to move from one place to another place: *We travel to work by bus; I travel to New York every year because my brother lives there*

unit one thing or one part of something: *There are twelve units in my English book;* one piece of money: *The dollar is the unit of money in the USA; The euro is the unit of money in France*

vaccinations you have a vaccination because you don't want to have an illness or disease: *I'm going to a hot country. I'm going to have vaccinations for typhoid, tetanus and polio*

Activities

1   **Look at the story and find this information. How fast can you find it?**

   1   Who is the dinosaur picture by?

   2   What colour is the packet of tea?

   3   What time does the food arrive at the supermarket?

   4   When is the antiques festival?

   5   What is the manager's first name?

   6   What colour is Clinton's suit?

   7   What time does the supermarket open?

   8   What colour are the supermarket bags?

2   **Are these sentences true (✓) or false (✗)? Correct the false ones.**

   1 ☐ The dinosaur picture is on the 500 gram packet.

   2 ☐ The Twinings tea is £2.99.

   3 ☐ Clinton hasn't got any banknotes.

   4 ☐ At the start, Clinton has four one pound coins.

   5 ☐ You don't need vaccinations for the sixteenth century.

   6 ☐ Clinton likes burgers and fries.

   7 ☐ There aren't any dogs in Clinton's time.

   8 ☐ The time machine is one hour into the future.

3 Complete the sentences with words from the glossary.

1 In Britain people often eat cornflakes for _____.

2 Leonardo da Vinci was a famous _____ in the fifteenth and sixteenth centuries.

3 Over sixty _____ people live in Britain.

4 He gets up at the _____ time every day.

5 She collects magazines. She's a magazine _____.

6 My keys are in the _____ of my jeans.

7 Her new _____ has a grey jacket and skirt.

8 He always drives very fast. He's a _____ driver!

4 Do these comprehension tasks.

1 Why is Kate Hermann's picture famous?

2 What is the young woman in the supermarket wearing?

3 What is she taking from a box?

4 When are they going to get the packets with the dinosaur picture?

5 How much is the tea packet at home?

6 How much does Clinton pay for a one pound coin?

7 How many vaccinations does Clinton need?

8 What is the young man wearing?

9 What is Clinton wearing?

10 Where is the old man sitting in the police car?

11 Who are the police officers looking for?

12 What does the restaurant sell?

13 Where does Clinton put his jacket?

14 Where is his jacket after the two hours work?

15 How much does she pay him?

16 How much does Clinton want?

17 Why can't Clinton sleep?

18 What does Clinton buy from the supermarket?

19 Where is his time machine?

20 Why can't Clinton leave Britain?

5 **Look at these receipts from the supermarket. Which one is Clinton's receipt? Highlight all the things that are wrong in the others.**
* Think about the day, the time, the prices.

1

```
FOODCO
WALLBRIDGE 3

CORNFLAKES                    2.59
CORNFLAKES                    2.59
CORNFLAKES                    2.59
ENG. BFAST TEA TWIN.          1.99
BAG                           0.05
BAG                           0.05

TOTAL TO PAY                  9.86
CHANGE DUE                    0.14

01.08.14      09:12
```

2

```
FOODCO
WALLBRIDGE 3

CORNFLAKES                    2.59
CORNFLAKES                    2.59
CORNFLAKES                    2.59
ENG. BFAST TEA TWIN.          1.99
BAG                           FREE
BAG                           FREE


TOTAL TO PAY                  9.76
CHANGE DUE                    0.24

02.08.14      08:12
```

3

```
FOODCO
WALLBRIDGE 3
                              2.49
CORNFLAKES                    2.49
CORNFLAKES                    2.49
CORNFLAKES                    1.99
ENG. BFAST TEA TWIN.          0.10
KETCHUP                       0.10
KETCHUP                       FREE
BAG                           FREE
BAG
                              9.66
TOTAL TO PAY                  0.34
CHANGE DUE

08.02.14      08:12
```

4

```
FOODCO
WALLBRIDGE 3

CORNFLAKES
CORNFLAKES                    2.59
CORNFLAKES                    2.59
EARL GREY TEA TWIN.           2.59
BAG                           1.99
BAG                           0.10
                              0.10
TOTAL TO PAY
CHANGE DUE                    9.96
                              0.04

01.08.14      20:12
```

6 Select an ending.

1 ☐
Clinton can't go home. He can't find the remote control. He stays and gets a job in the restaurant.

2 ☐
Clinton goes to the restaurant. The remote control is on the floor. He gets the control and goes home.

3 ☐
Clinton can't find the remote control. Then he has an idea. Tilda Birdsong comes back. She is looking for the packet. She takes him home, but she wants all his cornflakes packets.

4 ☐
Clinton can't find the remote control. Then he has an idea. Tilda Birdsong comes back. But her time machine can take only one person. What happens?

5 ☐
Clinton knows a lot about 2014. He can't go home, but he knows the winner of the future big football games and about business. Clinton stays in the twenty-first century and gets very rich.

Other titles available in the series

Garnet Oracle — Level 1

The Collector

The Locked Room

The Watchers

Zoo Diary

Garnet Oracle — Level 2

Casualty!

Strawberry and The Sensations

Underground

The Visit

Garnet Oracle — Level 3

African Adventure

Life Lines

Milo

Sunnyvista City

Garnet Oracle — Level 4

The Case of the Dead Batsman

The Hitchhiker

Space Romance

A Tidy Ghost

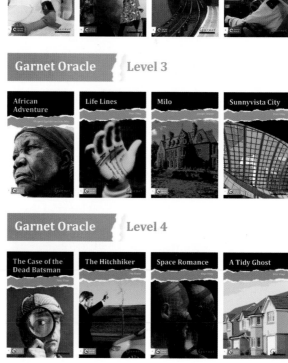